Wacky words compiled by Greg Lee
Daffy drawings made by Robert Court

The Rourke Corporation, Inc.
Vero Beach, Florida 32964

Lee, Greg, 1956-
    Food / Wacky words compiled by Greg Lee.
        p. cm. — (The little jokester)
    Summary: A collection of jokes and riddles about food, including
"Why would a pirate put a chicken where his treasure is buried? Because
eggs mark the spot."
    ISBN 0-86593-265-4
    1. Food—Juvenile humor. 2. Riddles, Juvenile. [1. Food—Wit and
humor. 2. Riddles. 3. Jokes.] I. Title. II. Series: Lee, Greg.
Little jokester.
PN6231.F66L44 1993
818'.5402—dc20   92-41730
                                                        CIP
                                                         AC

Produced by The Creative Spark
San Clemente, CA.

Customer: "Waiter, why is there a small bug in my salad?"
Waiter: "I'm terribly sorry. Would you like a bigger one?"

What does an anteater prefer on its pizza?
Extra antchovies.

What does Dracula get if he doesn't brush his teeth?
Bat breath.

What kind of food tells it like it is?
Frankfurters.

What did the apple say to the celery?
Quit stalking me.

Why does Dracula drink blood?
Because soft drinks make his teeth hurt.

How do doctors know that carrots are good for your eyes?
Have you ever seen a rabbit wearing glasses?

What does a hot dog say when it wins a race?
"I'm the wiener."

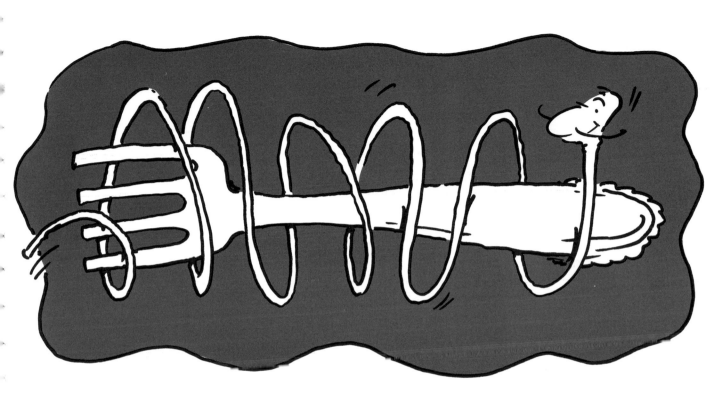

What do you get when you cross some pasta with a snake?
Spaghetti that winds itself on your fork.

What is Lassie's favorite vegetable?
Collie flower.

What do you get when you cross a centipede with a pig?
Bacon and legs.

What did the bowl of tapioca say when it won a million dollar
   lottery?
You're pudding me on.

Where does a grizzly bear sit when it goes into a
restaurant?
Anywhere it wants to.

What kind of vegetable should you always sit on before eating?
Squash.

Why did the baker suddenly quit his job at the donut shop?
He was sick and tired of the hole business.

What contains 47,000 pounds of dough and 26,000 pieces of pepperoni?
The Leaning Tower of Pizza.

What do ghosts like to chew?
Booble gum.

What do ants like to use for hula hoops?
Cheerios.

Jeff: "Did you know that horses like salad?"
Alicia: "Really, what kind?"
Jeff: "Colestraw."

What did King Arthur call his knight who loved steak?
Sir Loin.

Laura: "That fast-food chicken place is getting so expensive!"
Artie: "How come?"
Laura: "Yesterday I paid an arm and a leg for a wing and a thigh."

How do you make a strawberry shake?
Make it watch a scary movie.

How can you tell when there's an elephant in your refrigerator?
It's hard to shut the door.

What do monsters drink in the summertime?
Ghoul Aid.

Did you hear about the naughty boy who put a firecracker in the
    refrigerator?
He blew his cool.

Do hamburgers like to dance?
Sure, at the meat ball.

What did the broccoli say to the rotten lettuce?
"You should have your head examined."

What do witches order at a Chinese restaurant?
Misfortune cookies.

Why would a pirate put a chicken where his treasure is buried?
Because eggs mark the spot.

How does a ghost
lose weight?
It goes on a diet.

Assistant Chef: "How did you get that chicken on the rotisserie?"
Head Chef: "I told him it was a ferris wheel."

What's another name for a stolen yam?
A hot potato.

What did the bully say to the Thanksgiving turkey?
"I can beat the stuffing out of you."

What do you call a cow who gives you a hard time?
Beef jerky.

What's the difference between an elephant and a banana?
You can't pick up an elephant.

What is a vampire's favorite ice cream flavor?
Veinilla.

Customer: "I don't believe it! There's a bug in my sandwich!"
Waiter: "Not so loud ma'am, or everyone will want one."

Customer: "Waiter, what's this fly doing in my soup?"
Waiter: "I think it's the backstroke."

Did you hear the one about the frog who ordered soup in a
    restaurant?
He was *disappointed that there was no fly in it.*